Coptic Seminary   : Aughustinos Samaan

God the Word & Creation In Patrology

an introduction

Whatever I receive from me, I deposit it by honest people who are able to teach others (also (2 Tim 2: 2

The knowledge of the parents and their sayings makes us understand the Bible as if we heard it from God

2

I chose himself in this search by the grace
of God, God the Word, and the renewal of
creation in

Teach the fathers speaking from their
sayings on the dimensions of restoring
everything in Christ, our God, the Word,
explaining the concept of each and its
outcome.

Contents

5- The passages in which Saint Irenaeus mentioned our Mother the Virgin as a substitute for Eve:

6. The first Adam and the second Adam (Christ Jesus our God)

7. The contribution of our Virgin mother as a servant of salvation

According to Saint Athanasius, in response to the claims of
the Arians that the Son is not the Creator: -

When they say the saints who existed before the ages, they preach the eternity and immortality of the Son, and they mean this God Himself for that verses, it says (Isaiah 40:28): "The Eternal God is the Creator of the edges of the earth." And Susanna said: "O Eternal God" (Daniel (Susanah 42)) and confirms that (Heb 1: 3) "Who (the Son) is the radiance of his glory and the image of his essence".

It would be foolish to doubt the Son's being always (for he is the Creator of all creation)

And God said on Solomon's mouth, "Before the earth was created, before the depths were made, before the water fountains flowed, before the mountains were established, and before all the hills, they begat me" (Proverbs 8: 23-25)

The Father created by His word the Son all creation in the Holy Spirit

How do they separate them and claim that the son was a time when the claim was not present? This is not logically acceptable and bears the character of polytheism because the son in their minds is a human being and not a god or

an average god, and this is against our one true Orthodox
Christian teaching that we have received

And what I received from me, I deposited it with honest
people who are competent to teach others, and we will
deal in this paper with confirmation of the creation of the
Son for creation, and therefore it exists before its
existence, and the Creator is with

The Son is what is eternal, because the Son is in the Father
and the Son is in the Son, through the texts of the Fathers

Teachers who made disciples of all true Christians in all the
(world (1

Saint Athanasius the Apostolic - Dr. George Awad - (1)
second edition - November 2013, pp. 72 and 73

2- The renewal of creation according to Saint
Irenaeus: -

The first to use the term Recapitulation
ανακεφαλαιωων - meaning the restoration and
consensus of everything based on basic verses

Because "you do not commit adultery, do not kill, do
not steal," do not bear false testimony, you do not
desire you. (Rom. 13: 9) We were created again with
love, and through love, you are able to carry out the
commandments, so how can you commit adultery
with a woman if only if you take revenge on her
husband or do not respect her or do not respect and
love yourself, and so are the rest of the
commandments

"Likewise it is written also: Adam, the first man,
became a living soul, and the last Adam became a
living spirit. But not the spiritual first but the animal,
and after that the spiritual. The first man is from the
earth, earthy. The second man, the Lord, is from
heaven. As he is the earthy, so are the earthly ones
also. And as is the heavenly one, so also are the
heavenly ones. "(1 Corinthians 15: 45 -48)

Christ made us spiritual, so he renewed our creation
heavenly so that when we sin we resort to heaven for
God the Creator. This happened in the incarnation of
God the Word, Jesus Christ. One of two natures is a
complete humanity and a complete theology.

To arrange the filling of times, to bring together
everything in Christ, that which is in the heavens and
that which is on the earth, in that

In whom we also obtained an inheritance, predetermined according to the intention of the one who does everything according to the opinion of his will,

Let us be to the praise of his glory, we who have previously sought in Christ. (Eph 1: 10-12) God brought us together in His person, so that a name might be glorified in us (2) Just as sin entered into the kingdom of death through the disobedience of one man, and through the obedience of one person, he entered righteousness and brought forth the fruits of life in the people who died before, even though the first Adam was brought from the earth by means of The Word of God It was necessary that the same word of God regenerates Adam with his birth similar to him]) 3)

Luke in (The Genealogy of Christ) implies that the Lord has restored in his person all the nations that were dispersed from Adam, but all tongues and all generations of people, including Adam himself. That is why Paul calls Adam "an example of the coming" (Romans 5:14) because the Word is the Creator of the universe All of them had already been set as an example in Adam for the management of the incarnation that the Savior was about to complete. Because the Savior was present, he who would be saved must also come into existence so that salvation would not remain without his reason for existence ((4) God Jesus favored the whole world by himself in the Trinity(2) H. Lasiat, Promotion de l'homme en Jesus –Christ d'apre's Irenee deLyon, Meme P. 283 (3) Against Heresies - Saint Irenaeus (3:21:10)

As the father of the Church tradition recalled, Saint Irenaeus (The relationship is so close between man and the incarnate Word that we find between them a kind of exchange regarding the concept of the whole of the image, so man was created in the image of God, meaning the image of the word, and the complete in turn was incarnated in the image of the human being as a whole, showing in himself the truth of how man Created in the image of God, and this exchange, which is rooted in the creation of Adam, also serves to "restore everything in Christ" in terms of returning to the original (5)

And Saint Irenaeus was the first to introduce also the eschatological meaning of restoring everything by pushing human time to meet the Lord of time (6)

On the contrary, the prince of evil, Satan will also gather in him every sin and deceit, so that all the power of apostasy gathers in him the killing with him in the furnace of fire. Therefore it is entitled to refer to the name of the beast with the number 666 because he collects in himself all the mixture of evil that was exacerbated by the toucan as a result of the apostasy of the wicked angels, and he will combine Also in himself all the delusions of idolatry after the Flood (7)

In this way, he completes the concepts of restoring everything with the formative and moral dimension and the salvific dimension by completing the redemption and eschatology by meeting the Lord of glory on the Day of Judgment and this is the history of salvation and at the center of these three dimensions we find the meaning of time and the relationship between the time of human history and the eternity and eternity of God (8)

3- The salvation of man is achieved by: -

Belief in God the Father

Belief in the Son of God

Faith in the Holy Spirit (9) He does the commandments of God, baptism and works, and above all, he is supported by grace

(Against the Heresies - Saint Irenaeus (3: 22: 3 (4)

B.Sesboue , Tout recapituler dans le Christ , Christolgie et (5)soteriologie d'Irene' de Lyeon , Jesus et JC , P.150
B.de Margrgerie :Saint Irenee ,Exegete ecclesial de la recapitulation Christocentrique extrait de Id Introduction a (6)l'histoire de l'exegese.1980

(Against the Heresies - Saint Irenaeus - (5: 29: 2 (7)
(Against the Heresies - Saint Irenaeus (5 (8)
B.Sesboue ,Tout recapituler dans le Christ ,Christologie et soteriologie d'Irenee de Lyon ,P.171
9)Meme source

4- How do we obtain the new creation through baptism
and the Eucharist:

When a person asks for voluntary death in the sacrament
of baptism, they are reconciled with death (Romans 6)
They received the down payment of the Spirit and with the
new birth the believers received the gift of the Holy Spirit
An analogy with the breath of life. The Church itself is a
gift of God. We have entrusted it as he did to the breath

Life is the work of the hand of God, so the goal is that all
members metabolize it, they live in the church

It is placed in it the fellowship with Christ our God and the
Holy Spirit our God, and he is a token of corruption and he
too

It confirms our faith and it is the ladder of the ascension to
God. We are now receiving a certain part of the Holy Spirit
towards perfection

And the willingness not to corrupt. The deposit that stays
in us makes us spiritual until now and the mortal swallows
from

He says, "As for you, you are not in the flesh, but in the
spirit, for the Spirit of God dwells in you" (Romans 8

This does not happen when the flesh is thrown away . (9 :
but with the fellowship of the soul as he writes to his own
people

A flesh, but they took the Spirit of God, "which we cry out,
Father, Father" (Romans 8:15), and now that we have it

The deposit and we cry: O father, father, how will our
condition be when we rise and see him face to God's face
?and everything

Members will shout songs of rejoicing and glorify the One
who raised them from the dead and gave them eternal
.life

If the deposit is to collect all for himself and make him say,
"?"Abba, Father, then what will perfect grace work for

To the soul, which God will give to human beings? It will
make them like him and the will of God will be fulfilled,
and it will make

Man is in the image and likeness of God, and taken
through baptism, working towards our perfection, and
preparing us for nothingness

Corruption when they are able to expand and carry God.
The believers will not convert spiritually from now
And they pray to God "the Father of the Father" not by
rejecting the body but by reviving the soul to the body.
Perfection will be in me

The time to rise again is after death, because the soul will
fully revive the body and take over the soul
So that man can see God and her revelation in the face of
God through the full grace of the spirit can be
To be an image and likeness of God. The fruit of this
deposit found in baptism culminates in
Communion and the life in death that began in baptism
reaches its climax in an offering
Our death as the sacrifice of communion. (St. Ignatius,
Bishop of Antioch, quoted from Irenaeus's description, "I
Wheat for Christ I grinded with the teeth of predatory
(animals until they became the pure bread of God. (10

Ignatius of Antioch ,Rom .4.1. cited by Irenaeus ,
Eucharistic framework for understanding martyrdom is
also in The Martyrdom of Plycap , Where the structure of
(10)the narrative closely parallels that of the last super

. . The first Eve and the second Eve (Our Mother the 4
- :(Virgin Mary

As it has already been noted, restoring everything takes
place through one of the dimensions, which is the
dimension

The second is salvific and leads in turn to a consensus
between the science of proto-science (the science of
origins

Human), eschatology (eschatology), and anthropology (the
science of research about

The human being) through the Bible where the divine call
to man will find an integration of linking

Our mother the Virgin Mary in Eve, how? This is evidenced
by the interpretive cheek of the saint

Irenaeus, through the numbers of verses in which the
Apostle Paul emphasizes genealogy

Our God, Jesus, from the human point of view, and who
preceded him in the system of creation, resurrection, and
from it
Galatians 4: 4) "But when the fullness of time came, God)
sent His Son, born of a woman, who was born
Under the law
Rom 1: 3-4) "On the authority of his son, who became a)
descendant of David as far as the flesh is concerned, and
.named the Son of God

With power in terms of the spirit of holiness by the
" .resurrection from the dead

Rom. 9: 5) "They have the Fathers, including Christ)
according to the flesh, who is a blessed God over all

Forever Amen

In it, the descendants of Christ and the return to Adam and Eve are mentioned, and here Saint Irene does not only reside

Just an extension of the Pauline parallel between Christ - and Adam? Is not it an explanation of the Virgin

The New Eve - A Shared Provision of Salvation actually clarifies the vision

Pauline is about reformulating in Christ and understanding the role of reborn humanity in

The management of salvation and Saint Irene's understanding of the role of the reborn mankind in the management

Salvation by resorting to the chapters of the Gospels of the childhood of our God Jesus, which present our Mother, the Virgin

Mary, the fiancée of Joseph, is a virgin and obedient, but illuminates Pauline teaching and emphasis on Mary

As a reason for salvation as the steps to obtaining salvation, God united with his divinity

Two bodies, including (11) and the lawyer for Eve (12), and
this was shown in 65 passages of writings

Irenes

The passages in which Saint Irenaeus mentioned our -5
- :Mother the Virgin as a substitute for Eve
Who wrote against the heresies 1 3 and 4: 3 and 4 and 5
and 3: 5 and 4: 7 and 11 and 19 and 21 and 22 and 33 and
40 (13) in Latin (14) in the Armenian language

For Saint Irenaeus - Against Heresies - 3, 22 and 4 (11)
Saint Irenaeus - Against Heresies - 5 and 19 -1 (12)
Traduscion ,A.Riusseau,L.3:Sc210et 211(1974) ,L.4:SC
100(1965) etL.5:SC 152et 153(1969).Edition en un
vol.A.Rousseau ,Irenee de Lyeon ,Comtre les heresies
,denunciation et refutation de la gnose au nom menteuer
(13),paris,le Cref,1984
Demonstration de la predication Apostolique,intr.et notes
(14)par A.Rousseau ,Sc ,le Cref 1995/(Cite:DA)

∴ The first Adam and the second Adam (Christ Jesus our 6
- :(God

When the Apostle Paul affirms, "When the time was
fulfilled, God sent his Son, born of a new-born woman
Under the law (Galatians 4: 4) it reveals the new state of
adoption, those who are redeemed from the law

With the Son, Saint Irenaeus inquired about the new birth
and affirmed the birth of our Lord Jesus

Physically, it is a restoration of the birth of Adam

In this, the scholar Anises Jarasson says, "From his birth,
from Mary's womb, at that birth

By it Christ and his mission were fulfilled. The Lord Jesus,
son of Mary, restored life to humanity that was united

(In her a close union in Mary's womb. '' (15

That one of the blessings of the incarnation is life in God
and the basis for the completion of the redemption
process, and this is not counted

It is strange because our Lord and God Jesus is the son of
David, the son of Adam, and the son of God
The contribution of our Virgin Mother as a servant of -7
salvation (the saving dimension in the renewal of
- :(creation
- :A) Obedient virgin
The purity of the Virgin Mary and her obedience and
obedience to God were among the reasons for her
.selection as the mother of God the Word

Because as by the act of a disobedient virgin, man was
wounded, fell, and died, so by the act of the virgin who
obeyed the word of God, man was revived and through
(15)life, he gained life and thus she became Eve's advocate
The Marian Concept by Saint Irenaeus, Doctor of Theology,

Lyon - Baki Lyon Press, May 1932 - p. 89 (16) Against Heresies - Saint Irenaeus 3, 9, 2: 3, 16 and 2 B) Immaculate viscera that reborn human beings in God: -

The repository of the union of the word of God has united by itself a living body, which united nature into one nature

Unmixed in him, mankind was born again and he is still the powerful God who gave birth to him

Above description, St. Ambrose (17) found another aspect, which is that the Church was born

On the part of Christ while he was bleeding on the cross and between Eve, who was born on the part of Adam who slept on

(This thought was supported by Saint Jerome (18

C) Our Mother the Virgin Mary, Advocate of Eve: - As a result of her motherhood, she is called the Mother of God, not only to Eve, but to humanity especially at the cross
Mary participated in the provision of salvation by faith) and obedience) and for this she was called Eve's attorney (And because she bore God, she works for Eve (19

But St. Irenaeus remained silent about the role of Our Mother Virgin Mary in the eschatology (end times).

About Luke-2 and 87, the BJ Minni group. Latin (17)
Fathers -15-year 1585
Acts of Saint Jerome - Amy Martin - Paris Auguste (18)
Derry - 1838 - Latin Fathers 23
Against the Heresies - Saint Irenaeus-5, 19 and 1 (19)

8

8. The resurrection of God and the novelty of creation:

The disobedience of the first Adam led to punishment, and the obedience of the second Adam achieved justice and mercy together and was reformed

Creation, and God the Word, preserved in himself those who could not save themselves, and it was linked to Saint Irenaeus

Between the two natures of the theological word and humanity together, there is a strong response to the Gnostics and a similarity with him in that

Scholar Tertullian (20)

This was confirmed by Pope Kyrollos, the pillar of religion (21).

Saint Gregory the Theologian

+ Christ rose from the dead, so rise up with him.

+ Christ has returned and settled in his place, so you go back with him.

+ Christ was freed from the bonds of the grave, so you set free from the bonds of sin.

+ The gates of Hell have opened, and death is unraveling.

+ The old Adam turns away and the new one comes back to us.

+ And if there is a new creation in Christ, you will be renewed.

+ The Passover the Passover of the Lord. This is the feast of feasts and the season of the seasons, for it is above all festivals and gatherings, and it is preferred over all other feasts, as is the sun over other planets. Today we celebrate the Resurrection itself, which is no longer a hope and hope, but a living reality and a constant joy in our victory over death. It included the whole world

Tertullien, Contre les Valentinies, I, ed.J.Cl. Fredeouille, Sc280, paris 1980 (20)Adoption plutot que divisinsation, terme que Cyrille, a la difference d'Athanase, n'aime gure employer, et qu'Irenee 'n'emploie pas non plus. (21

+ And when Christ ascends to the heavens, then ascend with Him, and be with the angels. Helping to raise the doors to receive the one who comes from pain with kindness.

+ And answer the questioners: "Who is this King of glory?" Answer that he is the Lord God, King of glory, and "He is the strong and mighty Lord."

+ O riser, if we deservedly reach the desired goal, and become accepted in the heavenly recollections, we will offer you with the correctness of determination sacrifices acceptable to your holy altar.

O Father, Son, and Holy Spirit,

+ Because it is yours that all glory, honor, and authority shall be perpetuated forever.

Saint Polycarp, Bishop of Izmir

+ In one of the sermons of St. Polycarp, Bishop of Izmir (2nd century), it was stated about belief in the Resurrection of Christ and its result on the life and behavior of the believer:

Tighten your friends and fear God with fear and truth, throwing aside the empty talk of gossip and the delusion of nations, consolidating faith on those who raised our Lord from death, brought glory to him, and gave him a throne on his right. "He subjugates all that is in heaven and on earth," and everyone in him gives him the breath of life. And when he comes to "judge the living and the dead," whoever refuses to believe in him will be judged for his blood.

"He who raised him from death" will raise us with him also if we obey his will, follow the path of his commandments, love what he loves, and leave us all offense, greed, gossip and false testimony, and about the love of excessive money avoiding confronting evil with evil, insulting, and a blow with a blow, and a curse with a curse, citing teaching Who said: "Do not be judged, lest you be judged, forgive, be forgiven you, have mercy and have mercy. By the measure that you entrust you will be entrusted to you. Blessed are the poor and those persecuted for the sake of righteousness, for they have the kingdom of God." (22)

Saint Augustine: -

Our Lord has granted us His singular death (that is,
the death of his body without his own dying, because
his divinity did not leave his body nor his soul, but
rather the soul left the body and became the body
dead) This happened in exchange for our double
death in order to grant us a double resurrection ...

(A) Secret

(B) An example, for his one resurrection.

+ The Lord never sinned, nor was he evil, meaning he did not die in the spirit until he needed to renew the inner man calling for a life of righteousness with repentance. Rather, as he was wrapped in a mortal body, he died in the body alone (without dying a spiritual death) and by him also he rose and in his singular resurrection and gave us our double resurrection (i.e. resurrection) Our souls from their death and the resurrection of our bodies from their death, as by his resurrection:

(A) He made a secret about our inner being.

(B) He made an example with her regarding our external person. Singles

Because his dead body rose, but his soul never died because there is no evil in it. Therefore, it did not need reconciliation or resurrection. Rather what happened in the resurrection is that the living soul returned to his body that died by separating the soul from him and his resurrection became singular, but we need a resurrection of the dead soul and a resurrection Flesh (23)

(22)
http://www.coptology.com/Spirit/FR_Says_Easter200 7.html

http://www.avamena.com/vb/t5570.html\ (23)

From the biblical text of the Bible and from the sayings of the fathers received, we clearly understand the three dimensions of creation

It is the first creation on the day the universe was created, then Adam and Eve after it

Renewal of creation in the Incarnation, Redemption and Resurrection

The other dimension is the constant understanding of God when we are with him, and he says to us, "34 Then

The king says to those at his right hand: Come, Blessed Father, inherit the kingdom prepared for you.

Since the founding of the world.

35 For I was hungry, and you fed me. I was thirsty, and you gave me enough. You were a stranger, so you took care of me.

36 You clothed you naked. You are sick and you win me. Locked up, you came to me.

37 Then the righteous will answer him at that time, saying, O Lord, when we have seen you hungry, feed you, or

Thirsty and booed you?

38 And when did we see you as a stranger, and in you, or naked, and clothed you?

39 And when did we see you sick or imprisoned, and did we come to you?

40 So the king will answer and say to them: The truth I say to you: What you did to one of my siblings: 34 - These younger ones: (34)

By the intercession of the blood of our Lord and God Jesus, the Mother of Light, Mary, and all the ranks of angels and saints, Amen

Source: The Bible

References

Saint Athanasius the Apostolic - Dr. George Awad - second edition - November 2013

H. Bassiat, Promotion de l'homme en Jesus –Christ d'apre's Irenee de Lyon

Against Heresies - Saint Irenaeus

B. Sesboue, Tout recapituler dans le Christ, Christolgie et soteriologie d'Irene 'de Lyeon, Jesus et JC

B.de Margrgerie: Saint Irenee, Exegete ecclesial de la recapitulation Christocentrique extrait de Id Introduction a l'histoire de l'exegese

Ignatius of Antioch, Rom. 4.1. cited by Irenaeus, Eucharistic framework for understanding martyrdom is also in The Martyrdom of Plycap, Where the structure of the narrative closely parallels that of the last super

Traduscion, A. Reusseau, L.3: Sc210et 211 (1974), L.4: SC 100 (1965) etL.5: SC 152et 153 (1969). Edition en un vol.A.Rousseau, Irenee de Lyeon, Comtre les heresies, denunciation et refutation de la gnose au nom menteuer paris le Cref, 1984

Demonstration de la predication Apostolique, intr.et
notes par A. Rousseau, Sc, le Cref 1995 / (Cite: DA)

The Concept of Mary in Saint Irenaeus Doctor of
Theology Lyon - Bucky Lyon Press May 1932-p.89

About Luke-2 and 87, the BJ Minnie group. The Latin
Fathers -15-year 1585

The Works of Saint Jerome - L Amy Martin - Paris
Auguste Derry - 1838 - Latin Fathers 23

Tertullien, Contre les Valentinies, I, ed.J.Cl.
Fredeouille, Sc280, paris 1980

 Adoption plutot que divisinsation, terme que Cyrille, a
la difference d'Athanase, n'aime gure employer, et
qu'Irenee 'n'emploie pas non plus. (21)

(22)
http://www.coptology.com/Spirit/FR_Says_Easter200
7.html

http://www.avamena.com/vb/t5570.html (23)